80 Creativity Tips

Jen Nipps

Published by JEN Enterprises
Ada, Oklahoma

Jen Nipps

This book is manufactured in the United States of America.

ISBN-13: 978-0615796482
ISBN-10: 0615796486

JEN Enterprises
Jen Nipps
Ada, Oklahoma
www.jen-nipps.com

Orders: jen@jen-nipps.com

Dedication

There are many people who must be mentioned in this dedication. Forgive me if I don't name names.

To my parents who encouraged my own creativity.

To my friends who never laughed at my theories, mainly that everyone is creative but not everyone knows how to tap into it.

To the Writers' Colony at Dairy Hollow in Eureka Springs, Arkansas, for providing time and space where much of this book took shape.

To Crescent Dragonwagon for being a cofounder of the Writers' Colony.

Table of Contents

Jen Nipps

Introduction

Sometimes good habits worth keeping are difficult to establish and take some practice. In the long run, the habit makes it worth the time and difficulty.

Is enhancing/tapping into your creativity important to you? Did you think it would be something you could do without any work?

Creativity without work is what people sometimes call inspiration or the muse. Yes, that makes it fun, but it doesn't necessarily make it consistent or allow you to improve in whatever form of creativity you are working on.

I have included pages for you to take notes or doodle on. Once you've bought it, it's your book. What you do with the blank pages (and even the ones with text) is up to you. I've also included some pictures I have taken. Some illustrate a point of one of the tips. Some are just because. I have tried to keep the "just because" ones to a minimum and have tried to include only ones that complement one or more of the tips.

Enjoy!

Jen Nipps

Shoji screen

Go for a walk.

In her books, *The Right to Write* and *Walking in This World*, Julia Cameron encourages all artists, be they writers or painters, dancers or sculptors, to go for a regular walk. This isn't one of those power walks. This is meant to be a casual stroll through your neighborhood, a park, downtown, or in the woods.

Although, I do have to admit, it does have the added benefit of getting your exercise in. (The irony that I am eating potato chips while writing this is not lost on me. I will get my walk in later.) What are you to do on these walks? Think. Or don't. Observe. Or don't. Use the time to muddle through a creative problem. Or don't.

You get the idea.

Your mind will wander where it needs to go as your footsteps take you from your house to your neighbor's garden to the stop sign at the corner and so on.

I would suggest that you leave your earbuds at home. There are two reasons for this: First, if you're listening to music, you're telling yourself that you aren't willing to just observe or work on a creative conundrum or even spend time with yourself. You are worth the time to spend with yourself on your walks. Second, if your mind is wandering, you need some part of you to remain aware of your surroundings and your safety. After all, it's hard to do much creating if you're in a body cast because you wandered into the path of a car that couldn't stop in time. You can always listen to your music during your power walk later.

So—

When are you going for your walk?

Look at the sunset.

I love sunsets. There is something about the array of colors and the majesty of them that almost literally take my breath away. I think everyone, whether they think they are creative or not, needs to look at as many sunrises and sunsets as they possibly can.

The need to describe them may well drive you to do something creative. That "something" may be as simple as frying an egg and recognizing the pinkish covering over the golden yolk is a color from that morning's sunrise or the sunset from the previous evening.

A few years ago, a friend commented that she didn't feel like writing anymore, that she had sued up all of her creativity. Knowing how busy she stayed doing things for her students and family, I had one question for her. "How long has it been since you did something *just* for you?"

She thought for a minute and said, "I don't know."

"Here's what you need to do," I said. "Go outside tonight and watch the sunset. Even if it's just for one minute, that's one minute that is only for you and no one else."

She nodded. "I think I'll do that."

This conversation took place after a writers' group meeting we both attended. I had no way of knowing if she would do as I suggested or not. It was meant as a little advice, friend-to-friend, that I thought might be a little inspirational, at the very least.

At the meeting two weeks later, she said, "I have something I would like to tell the group." She looked at me. "Is it all right if I tell it?"

"It's yours to tell."

She told them about our talk, then said, "And do you know what? It works! I watched the sunset that night and it was absolutely magnificent! I just had to go in and write!"

I can't claim that watching a sunset—or sunrise—will have as dramatic of an effect for you as it did for her, but there's no denying that, at the very least, they're beautiful.

With that in mind, when is the last time you watched a sunset?

Take a shower.

Water and creativity seem to be inextricably connected, to me. Someone needs to invent a waterproof pen and waterproof paper or a waterproof recorder for times when people are in the shower or bath and get a wonderful idea that will be lost the very second they step foot out of the water.

No, it doesn't always happen that way. Many times, we do remember our water-borne ideas.

Why does it work? Let's be honest: There is no need to question the how and why of something working; just know that it does. (That said, though, I still want to know how and why. I'm sure I'm not the only one.)

Unless it is stagnant, water is always moving, always changing. Always adapting to its surroundings. Nothing man-made can contain, change, or shape it permanently. It's only temporary. The fluid and changing matter of our own creativity should remind us of this. We paint. It changes. We sing. It changes. We write. Again, it changes. This is good.

Taking a shower is one act of constant change. The water never hits you exactly the same way twice. The drops of water seem to reach deep within and massage ideas from the unconscious to the surface where we can reach them easily.

Don't worry about the ones you didn't remember. Even the best fisherman has his story about the one that got away. And he doesn't even know about the ones that swam by his hook and didn't try to bite.

Here's something I like to do—if I can—when I find myself in need of ideas:

Turn the shower on warm. Try to avoid too hot or too cold because then you only want to hurry and get done with the shower.

Get in and stand directly under the stream. (Yes, that means you have to get your hair wet.)

Close your eyes and feel each drop of water roll down your scalp and into your ears or down your forehead.

Don't think. Just feel. Soon, the ideas will start coming. Stop after you get a couple good ones.

Get dressed and either write your ideas down or get started on one immediately.

You might have found your personal *Moby Dick*.

Wash dishes.

Here we are with water again. This time, we're only getting in up to our elbows.

I know with the advent of dishwashers, we don't really do dishes much anymore, especially when we think about those super-wash models where we don't have to worry about rinsing dishes to get rid of that stuck-on yucky stuff. In that vein, you could well be thinking "What does washing dishes have to do with being creative?" and I can't blame you.

Bear with me and let's travel back in time to the days of the original dishwasher: Human beings.

We would stand with our hands elbow-deep in warm, soapy water. Wash and rinse plates, bowls, glasses, pots and pans, and knives, forks, and spoons. Feel the ebb and flow of the water. Hear the splish as we washed plates and the splash as we poured water out of cups and glasses.

As a child, I hated doing dishes. It was one more chore I didn't want to do. While I can't say I exactly like washing dishes by hand as an adult, it is more palatable. It gives me one more chance to do something I don't have to think about a lot.

My mind is free to work on other things. More often than not, my thoughts turn to poetry when I'm washing dishes. The rhythmic wash and rinse, ebb and flow, splish and splash mimic the natural rhythm of even modern free-verse poems.

They, in turn, mimic the rhythms of life. In this case, it isn't so much a question of life imitating art or vice versa. It's recognizing it all has a place and can all be useful to us in our creativity, whether finding ideas or putting them to work.

Yes, even while washing dishes.

NOTES

Doodle.

It doesn't matter if you want to call it scribbles, sketching, or doodling, just as long as you are willing to do it. Nobody says it has to be good, but it can be.

The front cover of my notebook is decorated with one lonely flower in a pot that I drew on there a couple days ago. Even as I write this, I'm considering adding some hearts to it. Nothing says our notebooks have to remain sterile on the outside.

There is also nothing that says when we write, must only write and do nothing else. I frequently crochet when I write. Working a simple pattern lets me work out what's next. Doodling does too. You don't have to think about light placement, shading, texture, or contour when you doodle.

In fact, you shouldn't think about those things. Thinking about them, while good done in their proper time and place, turns doodling into a different activity entirely. When you're doodling, you want to have fun. It's more like free-writing or brainstorming. The activity itself is reason enough to do it.

Let's go back to doodling as a way of working things out. A few hearts and some spirals have joined the flower pot on the front of my notebook by now. It's not so lonely anymore and I figured out how to proceed in what I'm currently writing as well.

And, as with the doodle, it's form is not permanent. I can always add to it later if I think it is needed.

Doodles remind us not to take ourselves or our creativity too seriously. Have fun with what you are working on, no matter what it is.

And doodle if you find yourself getting too serious.

Always have a pen and notebook with you.

I cannot emphasize the importance of this enough. In fact, it should probably be the first page in this book. Since it isn't, I take it as a sign of encouragement that you have read this far.

You never know when you might encounter an idea you want to remember. It could be in the middle of the night when you wake up from a dream. It could be when you're out shopping for school clothes for the kids.

No matter when or where it is, you want to be prepared. Just having a pen in your purse or pocket isn't enough. You can't always find a piece of paper or a napkin and there's only so much you can write on your hand.

Yes, this means that sometimes you will have to decipher your midnight chicken scratch because you didn't want to turn the light on. (I completely understand that, by the way.) You will wonder if you meant to write "blug," as it looks like you did; "frog," which could be another interpretation; or "blog," as in to start a new one to chart your creative efforts.

Of course, it could also mean that you should pain, sculpt, draw, or act like a frog. Those are all worthwhile creative pursuits as well. I have nothing to offer for "blug," though. If it were me, I was probably dreaming about drowning. But it wasn't me, so only you know what it means. Maybe.

One more thing about having a pen and paper nearby: Don't think that just because you don't carry a purse (or that you carry a small one), you can't carry a notebook.

Going to the paper aisle of any store (including, but not limited to, Staples, Wal-Mart, and Dollar General) show you a wide variety of notebooks and sizes from those that will fit in your pocket up to those large enough to fit in a briefcase. Be realistic in what you think you can carry with you.

In choosing your notebook, don't let its size dictate the size of your ideas. It is, after all, just a method of capturing ideas so you can work with them later.

Ask "what if."

"What if" is a powerful tool in exploring your current creative project.

Suppose an artist has painted a quiet lake scene. He thinks he is finished, but he asks "what if?"

What if he put a rope swing on the tree branch that hangs over the water?

What if he put a dock out on the water and a fishing boat in the middle of the lake?

What if he put people in all of those places, too?

He has transformed a peaceful lake scene to a fun family vacation. And all he did was ask "what if?"

That isn't limited to painting. A writer can ask "what if?" and turn a murder mystery into a romantic suspense. A dancer could add a pirouette after a plié to change the choreography even a little bit and breathe new life into an old dance.

The possibilities are endless.

You could even ask yourself "what if I could do something that would make this box cake mix taste a little less like it came from a box?" That might send you to look at your pantry. You could add some vanilla extract, some cinnamon, or even some cocoa powder to jazz it up a bit. I do this regularly. My cakes taste better for it. You could also do the same to change up your daily routine. If you think you are not creative (a notion with which I would personally disagree), asking "what if" to mix your routine up might have a side effect of jostling a bit of creativity loose.
You never know what could happen until you try it. And you could be pleasantly surprised.

Until then, ask "what if," even if it's just on paper, and see what could happen.

Forget the rules.

No matter what you do, someone before you has come along and devised a set of rules. And someone else has added to it.

Sometimes, these are safety concerns. Other times, they serve to provide a sense of boundary so you know the parameters of what you are trying to do.

This can be helpful and oddly freeing. Everyone has faced the blank page—or canvass—and froze up. No one is immune to it, especially if they are a beginner. This is where rules are particularly beneficial. They tell you whether to use a pencil or pen, acrylic or watercolor, and so on.

But what about later, when you have created and grown and developed as much as you can within the confines of the rules? What do you do when they feel restrictive?

That is when you forget the rules.

Yes, the rules still exist. Yes, you are free to use the ones that work for you, ignore the ones that don't (as long as you're not putting anyone at risk), and even make up your own.

Forgetting the rules lets you put a bold red slash in the middle of your canvass and that as the starting point for your free-form painting. I did something similar.

Many years ago, someone told me I would never be any kind of an artist. I believed her. I admired artists, but never thought I could be one until I was recognized as and called an artist for my beaded jewelry.

That acknowledgment knocked all the rules loose in my head. I bought some small canvasses, inexpensive paint brushes, and acrylic paints. I let myself play with the bright yellow all over the canvass. Then I did some red waves and dots. In the middle, I painted the word "create" in bold, black letters.

I loved it! I was happy with it. At first, I had to call it "unart" since it didn't fit any of the rules I knew. Now, I call it "word art."

Don't be afraid to forget the rules in whatever way works for you and frees your creativity.

Play.

Too often we consider play the realm of children. How wrong we are! We could learn quite a bit from them.

When children play, there are very few rules. They run with nowhere to go except the joy of running. They climb on jungle gyms and try to go higher with each swing. They slide down metal or plastic slides and run around to do it again.

Don't get me wrong. You won't find me running, but I'm not scared of the swings.

Swing high, then higher. Get dizzy on the merry-go-round. Climb high up on the jungle gym (or monkey bars, whatever you call them). Don't get too caught up in worrying about getting hurt (I understand that is a concern, which is why you won't find me running).

There is only one rule: Have fun!

Bring that sense of fun, that joy, that happiness with you when you come back to whatever project you were working on. Even tasks at our primary jobs will benefit with a little fun infusion and lead to us doing a better job.

Whose boss wouldn't appreciate that?

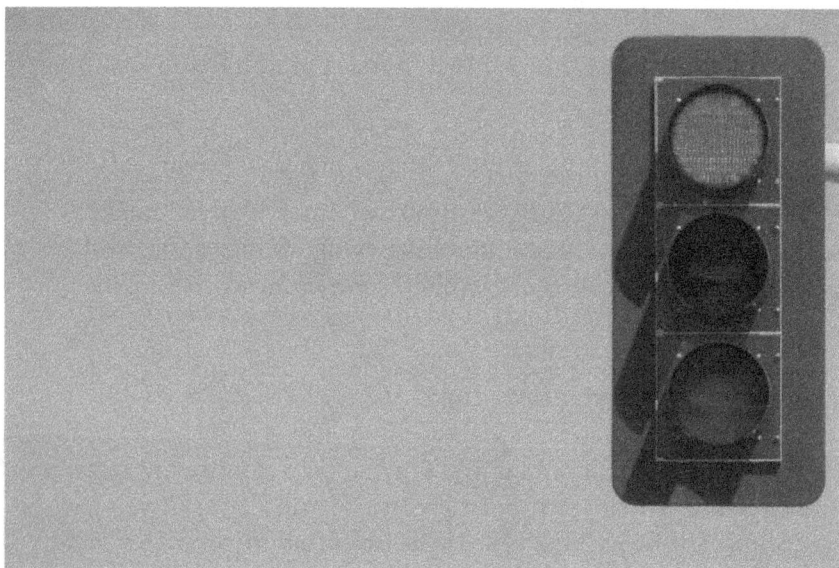

Stoplight

Take a nap.

Sometimes we just get too tired. When we are tempted to take a nap, we should do it, even if it's only 15 minutes. That's better than nothing.

When we get tired, we are easily distracted. Our creative work, which we usually enjoy, becomes hard and we want to quit. We get snappy, even with ourselves because we *know* we can do this! Back away from the project. Admit that you are tired and you want to take a nap.

Then go take one.

Fifteen to thirty minutes will help a great deal. Depending on what has been going on in your life, and if time allows it, an hour is better. If you don't sleep, then at least rest.

Later you can go back to your project without wanting to trash it.

Smell the flowers.

You're busy. You don't have time to work on your current creative project, though you really want to, but your daughter has to be at play practice, your son has to be at soccer practice, and your spouse wants to know what's for dinner.

Slow down!

It's time to smell the flowers. You don't have to be literal, but if you are, my favorites are roses and tulips, both of which smell nice.

What I really mean is, pay attention to details. That means you have to slow down so you can actually see them. Did you notice the wildflowers in the ditch alongside the road by the school when you took your daughter there for play practice? So there aren't any flowers at your son's soccer field. Did you notice the other parents? Have you thought about talking with them? Have you made a special point to spend time with your spouse so they don't feel neglected and start demanding things of you?

We all have busy lives. Sometimes we need to remember to stop and smell the flowers. It will carry over to your creative projects and the rest of your life.

Go outside.

I have my own private porch, balcony, or deck, whichever you want to call it. It's not very big, but it lets me get outside when I need to take a break. It lets me see—and hear—what the outdoors has in store for me. Today, I hear the wind rustling in the trees. A couple days ago, rain splashed down on the table and chair there.

When you were a kid, did your parents ever say, "Go outside."

Act as if they told you that now. Put on your shoes. Get away from the computer or TV. Put your book down.

Go outside!

There are numerous possibilities. True, you could do yard work while you're out there, but that isn't the point of this. Walk around. Touch things. Smell the air. See what's going on around you. Take it all in.

This is part of refilling your creative stores. We have to go outside once in a while so we can feel the sunshine on our heads and the wind in our faces. We have to reconnect with things that are not strictly man-made.

Going outside lets us do that.

Make a list of 5 things you like to do.

Generally, when we make lists, they are to-do lists on things that we really need to do or are grocery lists and don't have much to do with creativity.

Get pen and paper and number 1 through 5. List 5 things you like to do. Beside them, write when the last time was that you did it. If it's been a while, also list what you can do to start doing it again. For an example, here's my list:

1. Write. – I'm doing it now, so there isn't really a last time I did it. – I will likely write more this evening after dinner.
2. Crochet – A couple days ago. I ran out of one of the yarns for this project. – I bought more yarn and will work on that project later.
3. Listen to music. – Earlier today. – Sometimes I listen to music when I write, but sometimes it's a distraction—like right now—so I will listen when I crochet tonight.
4. Bake. – I made my dad a cake before I left for this trip. – I will make another cake for him when I get home in a couple weeks.
5. Take pictures. – Last week. – I have my camera with me and need to go outside and take some pictures. I will do that tomorrow.

Making such a list reminds us that there are things we can do that will enhance our creativity if we make time to do them. Start on an item on your list now.

Make a list of 5 things you don't like to do.

While we're making lists, let's do one more. This one, admittedly, isn't as fun.

Again, take pen and paper and number 1 to 5. This time, make a list of things you don't like to do. List the last time you did it and what you can do to get it done and marked off of your list.

I'll share my list again as an example:

1. Laundry. – Saturday. I had a bit piled up and needed to wash jeans. – Since it's just me here at the moment, I won't need to do laundry again until this coming Saturday.
2. Paying bills. – The first of the month. – I will pay them again at the first of the month. Being without electricity might force some creativity, but it wouldn't be very fun.
3. Shaving my legs. – I know I shaved them at the first of the summer. – I was supposed to buy a razor yesterday and forgot. I do feel more feminine with them shaved, so I'll have to make a special trip to get one tomorrow.
4. Washing dishes. – Yesterday. – Right now, there is only a saucer, a fork, and a spoon in the sink. I'll wash dishes after I add a few more to them tonight.
5. Exercise. – Friday. – I need to find something about exercise that's fun. I should have gone for another long walk today, but I am planning that for tomorrow.

Marking things off of our lists and getting things done has a side effect of providing us with a rush of momentum that we can then use in working on our creative project once the disliked task is done.

Jen Nipps

NOTES

Buy a box of colored pencils and use them.

Chances are, the last time you bought a box of colored pencils, they were on a school supply list for your kids. Haven't you ever wanted to buy a box for you, just for the fun of it?

Do it!

You don't have to buy a sketch pad or any special paper unless that's what you want to do. Regular printer paper works just fine. Take a few minutes just to play. Notice how the color can go from pastel to a vibrant swatch just by how much pressure you apply. If you're using printer paper, notice, too, how the texture of whatever is under the paper shows through.

Have fun playing with your colored pencils. Go by your own rules and make abstract art or disproportionate people or furniture.

Only you set the limits.

Don't listen to the "experts."

When you're starting something new, "experts" swarm like gnats on my morning walks. Each one has advice for you on how to do what you're doing. If you listen to them all and try to go by what they say, soon you find yourself stuck.

At the outset, the only expert you need to listen to is YOU. Why?

You are the only one who knows what it is you are doing and what you want to do. Otherwise, they're wasting your time and you're wasting theirs. The thing of it is, many experts don't see it that way. You will either need to convince them or ignore them. It might not be polite, but they're being a bit rude themselves, aren't they?

Once you have a direction in mind, you can read the articles and listen to the experts you want to listen to. It wouldn't do you much good to listen to a choreographer expert when you're drawing still-lifes or vice versa.

Here's another thing to consider: Some of the experts aren't experts at all. That is another reason to avoid them at the beginning. At that time, you have no way of knowing who is legitimate or not. Only experience will tell you that. Take time to do your homework when you're deciding on your direction and you'll be able to figure out which experts are truly experts and worth your time.

Trust yourself.

As creatives, we are often plagued with self-doubt and thoughts that our work isn't good enough, we don't know enough to do this, *we* aren't good enough.

Let me tell you, they're all wrong. While our *beginning* work might not have been good enough, it improves as we work at our craft, regardless of what it is. In order to continue working on it, in order to believe your work is good enough, there's something key that you need to do.

Trust yourself.

It's true we are our own worst critics, but we're also our own best advocates.

Just do it.

It is possible to talk an idea to death. I know. I've done it frequently with stories. There was a lesson I had to learn. I hope you won't have to learn it the same way I did.

I had a great idea for a story. It would be a fantasy novel. I would talk about it to writer friends and tell them about it. I would tell interested family and other friends about it. I would write a chapter or two and it would fizzle out.

Why?

I talked about it too much. I put so much energy and time into the talking about it that when it came time to write it, I had no more energy for it.

The same could be true of a painting or a new dance. How much time do you spend talking about it and how much time do you spend working on it?

Just do it!

Try something new.

Staying in one creative format all the time can lead to stagnation, frustration, and giving up on whatever it is you're doing. There are ways to combat this.

The primary—and most effective—one is to try something new. I don't mean to try a new technique or method. I mean something entirely new.

You paint, so learn to crochet. You write, so learn to sculpt. It stretches your creativity in ways that you can't do on your own while providing the discipline of creating so it doesn't get stale and you don't get out of the habit.

Think about it. What is something you have wanted to learn but haven't let yourself because you think you don't have time?

We make time for the things that are important to us. Make learning something new a priority and watch your creativity grow.

Jen Nipps

Storm Cloud

Cook.

Cooking is one of the original acts of creating. You take raw ingredients and make something entirely different from them. What is more creative than that?

One time, after I graduated from college, I was making a chicken and pasta dish. It was almost finished when I realized I didn't have *anything* for a sauce. I looked in the fridge and grabbed some milk, butter, and two pieces of sliced cheese. I heated the milk and melted the cheese and butter in it and made a semi-alfredo sauce.

Since then, I learned that using flour and butter to make a roux is the better way to go, but, honestly, I'm not sure I had any flour then. Remember, I hadn't been out of college very long.
I like to experiment in the kitchen. I don't do it very often because when I cook, it's generally for more people than myself. If I'm the only one who has to eat my mess, that's one thing, but I won't inflict an experiment-gone-bad on anyone else.

When is the last time you cooked? Did you see it as a chore to get through or an exercise in creativity? It's easy to see it as one more thing that has to be done in the course of a day. Challenge yourself to see it as another way to be creative.

Garden.

First, a caveat: I am not a gardener. My thumb is so brown, it's almost black. I tend to kill plants rather than grow them. And I have tried.

Remember when I said cooking is one of the original acts of creating? Gardening is another one. Delayed gratification is the name of the game here, though.

Having your hands in the dirt, planting, weeding, and tending connects you directly to the source of our creativity. You tap directly into the ultimate creativity when you garden.

At one time, my grandma had an extensive rose garden in her back yard. It was rare for her to have two rosebushes exactly alike. Gardening, and showing the end results, gave her joy and fed into other areas of her life, including, I believe, cooking.

Don't be afraid to get your hands dirty. They'll wash.

Dance.

Whether it's just swaying to the music, hip hop, jazz, ballet, or tap, dance has a rhythm all its own.

You don't have to be a choreographer to dance. In fact, for this exercise, it's probably better if you aren't. You won't be analyzing your moves for proper form and so will be able to focus on just having fun. That's the point.

Dancing both uses and creates energy. It uses pent-up energy that needs to be released. It creates energy you can use in your creative work.

No one's watching.

Dance.

Sing.

We don't have to have any special tools to create. We only need our own voice. With it, we can create music.

It doesn't matter if you sing a real song, make one up yourself, sing vocalizations, or hum. It's music. It's creating.

Some people sing in the privacy of their own home (we won't get into singing in the bathroom, though sometimes they do have good acoustics). Some sing in the church choir. Some have made careers—and became quite famous—because of their singing.

Sing for fun. Sing to create.

Draw.

A couple years ago, I had decided I was going to learn how to draw. I bought a book or two and set out to do just that. I don't know where the books are, but I remember the best thing to come out of that endeavor.

It's called a "wooly woo" or something like that.

Basically, you draw an oval in the middle of a page for the nose. Then you draw straight or squiggly lines (depending on if you want your creature to have curly or straight hair) and make him as fuzzy as you want. Then you color in the (black) eyes. Its mouth is hidden under all the hair.

It's cuter than you think it would be. And it's fun to draw it. There's no way to do it wrong.

In fact, unless you're taking art classes to learn to draw better, there's really no one to tell you if you're doing it wrong at all. If you like how it looks, that's the right way to do it.

Jen Nipps

NOTES

Begin at the bell.

A friend of mine said this before a writing exercise we did at the kick-off party/meeting for the local National Novel Writing Month (NaNoWriMo) group.

"Begin at the bell" is actually pretty good advice. When it comes to working on our creative projects, we almost always say we don't have time.

Make time! Otherwise, it will never get done.

Get a timer. Set it for no less than 15 minutes, preferably 30. If you can, have a bell ring to signal the beginning. If not, start the very second your hand comes off the timer.

Whatever it is you do, then do it. Write. Draw. Pain. Knit. Cook. Dance.

Create!

When the timer goes off, you can stop, but not before. Give yourself at least that 15 minutes. If you are going good when time is up, turn the timer off—or reset it—and keep going.

At the end of your time, step back. Look at what you have done and pat yourself on the back.

This is important. *Do not* evaluate or critique what you have done. Now is the time for creating, not for editing or judging. There will be time for that later.

Here are some tips for you on your work with a timer:

Don't look at the timer. Turn it away from you. If it's on your phone, turn the display off or turn your phone over.

Don't stop and wonder how much time you have left, no matter how much you want to know. Time isn't important except as a way to get started. Unless there's a hurricane or a fire, the amount of time that's passed isn't important.

If you're writing or drawing, keep your hand moving. Pause as seldom as possible to work out a muscle cramp if you need to. (As a side note, if you get cramps like that, it means you're holding your pen/pencil/paintbrush/knitting needles/crochet hook too tight and you need to loosen your grip.)

Focus on what you're doing. Is music or TV on in the background? Tune it out. There are people who say they *have* to work in complete silence. Those people rarely get any work done.

Distractions are a fact of life, even if it's just your cat jumping up on the desk. Learn to deal with it.

You're creative *in* your life, not separate from it.

Paint.

We're not talking about painting your living room walls here, unless, of course, you paint murals on them.

It is possible to buy canvas, brushes, and paint inexpensively at either a craft store like Michaels or Hobby Lobby or even at Wal-Mart. The price of your supplies isn't important. The fact that you buy and use them is.

Get your things ready so you don't have to keep getting up and down for a clean brush or a cup of water. Now what?

What do you want to do? What do you see on the blank canvas in front of you?

I've done this exercise in the past. I saw the canvas as bright yellow, so I painted it. I even painted the sides of the canvas so there was no white showing anywhere. I added wavy lines painted in red and dots between the lines. I wanted something more for the painting, so I added a word: "Create."

It was the first art I had painted since I was 12 years old. I liked it. I did three more in a similar way, using "Dream," "Believe," and "Imagine," as I went. In the beginning, I called it "unart." Then I called it "word art."

You don't have to paint something as abstract as I did. But you do need to paint to tap into a different stream of your creativity.

Write.

Although I advocate all types/outlooks for creativity, I primarily view myself as a writer. I have written books, articles, poems, short stories, and novels. I have written blog posts and journal entries. Over the years, I have had my words published in one form or another. Everything I have written has *not* been published. Some of it was writing just for fun and not meant to be in print. Some of it was not my best work and should not have been published for that reason.

I'm telling you this for one reason. First and foremost, write for *yourself*. If you never have anything published, that's okay. You need to have a place where you can write about your current projects, your thoughts about what you want to do, and your feelings about the process without wondering if anyone will ever read it. It also gives you a place to work out any problems you might be having.

Writing can *be* your creative outlet or it can be a cornerstone for your other creative projects. Only you can decide what role it will play in your creativity.

All I ask is that you be willing to free-write for 15 minutes a day. It's possible you might unlock a block you didn't know you had in the process.

"You can't wait for inspiration. You have to go after it with a club." ~Jack London.

Do you wait until you are inspired before you start to create? Why? Does it work for you? Do you get very much creative work done?

I used to wait to be inspired. I said my muse was fickle. Well… She isn't. She needs a schedule. A routine. When I set a routine of *consciously* creating every day, she shows up and we work wonderfully together.

A routine doesn't have to be a rigorous schedule. I daresay my muse would go on strike if I tried that. Some semblance of routine, such as sitting down to write after dinner, lets the muse know you're ready for her and she won't keep you waiting.

Make an Idea Pocket.

An Idea Pocket is an envelope (or part of an envelope) where you can carry items for inspiration.

Here's how you make one:

Take a standard #10 business envelops and seal the flap shut.

Cut off the top 1/3 of the envelope. (You'll be cutting the short side of the envelop.)

Put a label with a short nonsense poem on the front of the envelope.

My Idea Pocket

I want to write.
I want to draw.
Try though I might,
I can't think of anything at all!

I reach my hand in here
And find something very near.
It's just what I need!

I'll put it back or put in something new
So I can use it another time too.

Look through magazines and pictures for things to include in the pocket. When you're going about everyday life, if you see something you think would be interesting, put it in there as well.

A tip: When looking for pictures, try to avoid ones of people you know and/or of celebrities. You have preconceived ideas about them and might not be as open to the spark of inspiration as you might be otherwise.

How do you use it? Here's a tip: Don't over-think it.

Take your Idea Pocket and—without looking—pull something out. Look at it from all angles. Turn it over and look at the back, even. What colors are there? Shapes? If it's a picture, who are the people and what are they doing?

Don't question why you pulled that one out. Don't wish you had picked something else. Use it.

What is your creativity medium of choice? Does the item you picked out inspire you to do anything? What?

Do it. If it's writing, write. Drawing, draw. Cooking, cook or at least write out a recipe.

Creativity does not discriminate by age, race, religion, location, or form. Be open to it.

Plastic Eggs

Forget about being good.

I think it's hardwired into our DNA that we have to be good at what we do. Nobody wants to be a beginner. We take an interest in a new hobby and we want to be good at it *now*.

Julia Cameron and Natalie Goldberg both refer to a concept known as beginner's mind. In that state of mind, you forget about being good, forget about being the best, and enjoy the process of learning something new and stretching yourself in your creativity.

How do you get into this mindset? I don't know. Sometimes I can do it. Sometimes I can't. I do know this: If I can go into something only with the intent to have fun with it, whatever "it" is, I am more able to forget about being good and just enjoy the process.

Maybe that's the key.

Starting a new school year was always exciting—whether in anticipation or in dread—and that is an attitude we need to take with us to any new endeavor. Be excited about what you do and being "good" will follow soon enough.

"Someday" Is Now.

Too often, we make life all about what work we need to do. We relegate the things we *want* to do to the realm of "someday."
It's time to wake up and realize "someday" is now. It isn't after the kids move out. It's not after you retire. It's *now*. Schedule time to play. Do something you want to do.

By playing, we find our creativity. We find what we truly enjoy, what we love. Playing eliminates the barriers we put up when we have to work, be responsible, and act like the grown-up.
It allows us to access our creative stores. The well that Julia Cameron writes about in *The Artist's Way*. With enough practice, enough play, we will be able to access our creativity even when we are being responsible.. Then, when our boss comes to us wanting a creative solution to a situation and asks that we think outside the box, we are able to do that. We don't panic. We just do it.

By scheduling time to play and by making today into "someday", we find ourselves happier, healthier, better-rounded, and more productive in general.

Focus on your feet.

What, you might be wondering, does focusing on your feet have to do with being creative? There are a few ways.

They keep us grounded. We're all familiar with the concept of the flakey artist who spends more time in their head than in reality. If we remember to stay grounded, we avoid becoming that stereotype.

They can take us to new places or to places we seldom go. By going, *physically*, to these places, we see, smell, touch, hear, and maybe even taste things in a different way. It might be something we are already familiar with, but it's the different combination of those senses with the unfamiliar location that we will find beneficial. It will aid in replenishing our creative stores.

The can take us back to where we have been in the past. Sometimes we need to revisit parts of our past in order to move through creative blocks. Our feet can take us there and help us move forward once again.

And this is all because we took a minute to focus on our feet.

Allow imperfection.

A lot of times, we tend to think that what we're working on has to be perfect right out of the gate. If we are realistic with ourselves, though, we know that rarely happens.

Writers must revise and rewrite until they get something that might appeal to their readers. Painters tend to sketch and draw before they put brush to canvas. Dancers must determine the steps of their dance and practice before it is presentable.

Even Leonardo da Vinci kept sketchbooks. It would appear he did not even expect perfection from himself. Should we be any different with ourselves?

Take a picture of your progress.

We live in a society of instant gratification. We want it and we want it now.

If you're working on a large project, that isn't always possible. What is a creative person to do, short of never doing a large project ever again?

Take pictures of different stages along the way.

If you're so inclined, take a picture of every step. When you're done, not only will you have the large project complete, you'll also have a tutorial to either share with others or to keep for yourself for future reference.

That way, the picture progress would be beneficial in more ways, thus serving two purposes as well as keeping your motivation and creativity up.

Jen Nipps

NOTES

Editing as Creating

For many people, editing appears to be the antithesis to creativity. It is actually part of the creative process.

A different function of it, true, but that doesn't make it an opposite. As I see it, here are some of the processes to creating:

- o Generating the idea.
- o Planning/researching.
- o Creating (writing, composing, drawing, painting, etc.)
- o Revising/changing/adding

Revising and changing...editing.

No project is completed after the initial part is done. The bones of the story, for example, might be written down. It might even be fleshed out some.

The thing of it is, there is likely excess flesh in some areas and not enough in others. That's where the revising/changing/adding/*editing* comes in.

It's not something anyone should look at as being in opposition to the art of creativity. Instead, it should be seen as an important part of the process that should not be overlooked, ignored, or rushed.

Use the weather.

So now you think I'm off my rocker because I advocate walking in the rain, right?

That's fine with me. I've never made any claims to sanity and normalcy is vastly over-rated.

Seriously, though, we have to use things around us to help fuel our creativity, to keep the creative well filled and the pump primed.

One constant in life is weather. Whether it's sunny or cloudy, raining or snowing, the weather influences us. Some may hurt when the weather changes. Some may be depressed when it's winter and the days are shorter.

I'm solar powered. I love the sun. I can't be out in it long because I burn easily, but by my mood, even if I don't see it, I can tell you if the sun is out. Most of the time.

In our creative projects, we have to employ emotion. Use the weather, either figuratively or literally, to help you do that.

Walk in the rain.

We've already established that, for me, water is inspiring. I get ideas in the shower, elbow-deep in dishwater, swimming, etc.

If it's not raining hard and if it's not storming, I love to walk in the rain. I won't melt. I'm not that sweet.

The other day, it was raining. It was actually raining too hard to go walk in it. When is the last time you went walking in the rain?

Think back to it, or, if possible, go out and get into it. Don't use an umbrella. That doesn't count. You have to let the rain fall on your head, down your shoulders, for it to count.

Let the water seep in, refill your well, and energize your creativity.

Do something different.

Do something different *physically*. Chances are, you don't often lie on your bed with your head hanging over the edge like yesterday's exercise encouraged.

Doing things in a different way makes your brain work differently, establishing a different pattern. Different patterns, I have heard, awaken more parts of your brain and increase blood flow to your brain as well.

The idea, as I understand it, is you will be more clear-headed and more open to new things. That's how it needs to be with creativity. If you close yourself off to something because it's not what you usually do, you're closing yourself off to creativity in general. By physically moving differently, you use your brain differently and, therefore, stay more open, which is where you need to be.

Stand on your head.

Not literally, unless you want to.

When I was a little girl, I would lie on my back across my bed and let my head hang over the edge. My hair would brush the floor (it was long, then), and I would lie there until I felt a little bit dizzy and my tummy tickled. I'd laugh when I sat up because it made the room spin a little bit and my tummy tickled more.

What does that have to do with today's creativity exercise?

I want you to do that. Do it, then describe it. See what of that feeling, what of the act of lying down with your head hanging over the edge of your bed, you can use in your current project. In your description(s), don't be afraid to use "silly" words, like "tummy," "belly," and their like.

Jen Nipps

Bouquet Stars

Wander.

I've been needing to refill my well for a couple days. That's directly related to today's tip.

Wander.

Wander with purpose. Wander without purpose.

Just wander.

Whether you intend to or not, you'll be refilling your well; you'll be taking inspiration in with every step, every breath, you take. You can "wander" by daydreaming or by looking at picture sites online, but it's best if you can actually get outside and truly, physically wander.

Use your senses.

What are our senses?

- o Hearing
- o Sight
- o Smell
- o Taste
- o Touch

Using the senses can make your creative endeavors livelier. Some, of course, cannot be translated directly, depending on what form you prefer to work in, but they can still influence and inform what you do.

Paying attention to your senses and the information they provide will eventually make you a more observant and more creative person.

It isn't easy.

Like a physical exercise that requires you to stretch in ways you're not used to, it will be hard for a while. Over time, with consistent practice, it will get easier.

Stretch.

We are creatures of habit. We don't really like to do things that are outside of our comfort zone, physically or mentally.

Physical stretching isn't necessarily comfortable. Neither is mental stretching.

Creative stretching is even less comfortable, but just as necessary, if not more so.

Get out of your comfort zone and try something new. It could be the spark you need to re-start your creativity.

Get out of the house.

Your daily routine, regardless of how comfortable it is, could be hindering your creativity. You need to shake your routine up some. Get out of the house. Perhaps even get out of town.

If you're doing the same thing every day, you're not giving yourself any chances to refill your creativity reservoir, your well, your — pardon the obvious analogy — pocket.

Do something you like to do. Do something only for you. Spend time with like-minded people (such as at a workshop).

When you get back home, back to your routine, perhaps you'll have a bit of a spring in your step and be more ready to embark on your creative journey again.

Yes, you can.

You think this phrase isn't a creativity tip? It is. It's particularly useful when you are doubting yourself.

The other day, I was talking with a cousin I haven't seen in quite some time. Conversation turned to writing and the question came up about if I have been published.

She said, "I'd like to write, but it wouldn't be publishable."

My first reaction (that I did not say) was "So?"

My second reaction, which I did say, was, "You never know."

It's true. You don't know. What's more, because you tell yourself it wouldn't be publishable (or saleable, if you're talking in terms of visual art), you're telling yourself that you can't do it. You let your self-doubt win before you even try to start.

The thing of it is, very few people start out with the intent to be published. To think that way right out of the gate is like trying to win the gold medal in the Olympics the first time you jump off a diving board. You have to practice first. Then you start with small competitions (i.e. submissions/contests).

Only after you gain your confidence do you try to aim to be "published." You can't be afraid to try. And you certainly should never tell yourself that you can't and then don't even try.

Jen Nipps

NOTES

Give yourself permission.

I am not suggesting you have to ask anyone's permission before you can create anything.

Rather, you have to give *yourself* permission.

Give yourself permission to write, to draw, to dance, to cook. To imagine, to daydream.

To create.

Give yourself permission to write the worst drivel in the world, paint or draw the worst scribbles imaginable, cook the worst dish ever.

No, you *won't* do the "worst ever." But the act of giving yourself permission is twofold.

First, it starts to break down the walls you've built around yourself saying you can't because you "aren't creative." Second, it silences the inner you that says it's bad, wrong, ugly, etc.

Giving yourself permission to create and to do the worst frees you to do what you want. You can evaluate the results later.

Relax.

It's easy to become aggravated or frustrated when things don't work out the way we want them to. This seems especially true of creativity.

It didn't turn out how you wanted or you don't really know how to do it (this is true for me in terms of drawing).

Relax.

One of my "rules" for creativity is the only way you can do it wrong is to say you are. You can't expect perfection right out of the gate.

When you relax, you let go of your aggravation and frustration. When you relax, you have fun with it. That's the whole point anyway.

Take a hike (literally).

Sometimes to clear the cobwebs from our brains and get the blood flowing like it's supposed to so we can tap into our creativity, we have to get moving physically.

Take a hike. Come on, put those tennis shoes or hiking boots on and get going! It doesn't have to be for long.

While you're out, if you find any interesting rocks, twigs, etc., pick them up to put in your Idea Pocket later. (More about Idea Pockets in another tip.)

That's not the main point of this, though. While you're walking, be observant but don't put too much focus on any one thing. Take it all in.

At the end of your hike, what stands out to you the most? Write it, draw it, paint it, dance it...*Whatever* it.

Don't be afraid to scratch.

In her book, *The Creative Habit*, Twyla Tharp defines scratching as the search for an idea to get you started.

As you look for something to strike that creative spark, look to those that have gone before. If you paint, look at paintings you admire; if you write, read the masters or read authors you admire; cook, look in old cookbooks. The list goes on.

Don't worry that you'll inadvertently steal someone else's work. The spark you get from whatever you look at, from whatever you see or hear or do, will lead you in a different direction than the inspiration.

Go ahead. Scratch.

Exercise your mind.

Yes, exercise. Don't run away just yet. Hear me out.

Just like our physical muscles need to be worked to stay/get in shape, so does our creativity. Even though everyone is creative (and I firmly believe that), creativity is not something you can just turn off and on at command.

Several years ago, there was a Hewlett-Packard commercial with Gwen Stefani. She said something very similar to that. "It's not something you can turn off or on." (That may not be a direct quote. I haven't seen the commercial in quite a while.) She's very right.

While you're thinking of that commercial and Gwen Stefani's views on creativity, here's an exercise for you to try:

What is a product you use on a daily basis that you feel like you could not live without? What if you were asked to endorse it? What would you say about it to convince someone else to buy it?

Think outside the box.

DO NOT tell yourself you can't do it. Yes, you can.

Hint: It would help if you have a picture of this item in your Idea Pocket.

Candle Flame

Daydream.

Contrary to popular belief, daydreaming is not a waste of time.

Daydreaming is where we get some of our best ideas.

Try some directed daydreaming. Get a pen and paper or sketchpad. Sit down for a specific time (maybe just five minutes). Set a timer if you need to.

Go ahead.

Daydream.

You have permission. It's a creativity exercise.

Write or draw as you see fit during that time. Or do your writing/drawing after the timer goes off.

What did you come up with?

Ignore your inner critic.

Anyone who routinely engages in creative pursuits has an inner critic who judges what they do. Ignore them.

Lately, mine has been telling me that everything I write is trite, clichéd, and overused. It has been nitpicking my grammar and word choices.

It isn't easy to ignore your critic. Sometimes it has a good point and a legitimate complaint. Those times lure you into thinking they're good to keep around.

They aren't.

Unfortunately, they will never go away completely. There's an exercise you can do to silence them temporarily. You need a 3x5 index card and an envelope.

Draw a picture of your critic. If drawing isn't in your skillset, a stick figure is fine. (That's what I did.) Write down some of the things your critic says. Pay particular attention to the things that stop you in your tracks.

When you're done (using the back of the card is fine), exile your critic. Put it in the envelope and seal it. Write a release date on the outside of the envelope. Stick it in a drawer and forget about it. (Write the release date on your calendar.)

Now…

Get to work on your project and ignore the distant cries of your inner critic. They'll get to have a look at your work later.

Much later.

If something doesn't work for you, change it.

Take a look at your workspace.

Does it work for you? When you get ready to create, is it comfortable and welcoming? Are there too many distractions, be they man-made or environmental?

If something isn't working for you, change it. If that means moving to a new room, do it.

Forcing yourself to work in a location or under circumstances that don't work for you can be a boost to your creativity for a short time. Do it for too long, though, and you'll find yourself avoiding the work, the creating, and letting it stagnate. Be proactive to avoid that.

Take it slow.

I think part of the reason we experience creative blocks is because we have become conditioned to expect immediate results. So many of us are on the fast track that we don't know how to do it any other way.

Yes, I am including myself here

Slow down.

Creativity is a process, a way of life, not an end result. When we go too fast, we try to force our creativity.

It doesn't work like that.

If we are hitting our stride, in the zone, or whatever other sports metaphor you want to use, it's okay to go fast. Remember to be willing to slow down when it's time.

Your creativity is like a river-fed well. Sometimes it is near to overflowing. That's why you are able to work fast. Other times, the river feeding your well is sluggish and you feel like you're dammed up. It's most likely somewhere in the middle. Steady and letting you work at a reasonable pace.

That's the key word: reasonable. It probably feels slow compared to how you have worked before and how you would prefer to work. It's healthier for you in the long run and avoids burnout.

Give yourself permission to take it slow.

Be nosey.

I have a confession to make. I'm nosey. I like to know what's going on. I like to know how things work behind the scenes.

It has fueled my creativity more times, more ways, than I can count.

For example: On more than one occasion, I wondered what would – or could – cause seizures. I worked as a medical transcriptionist for 12 years. A chart came across my desk where someone started having seizures after a severe closed-head injury.

Bingo!

In the next story I wrote, I gave the main character seizures – or "falling fits" – after a head injury. Of course, I couldn't leave it at that, so he also lost his eyesight after another head injury during a seizure.

Obviously, you don't have to be that dramatic. Being nosey allows you to eavesdrop on conversations in public (like the couple who met online first then at a local restaurant where he was holding forth on how glad he was that she was how she presented herself – shallow jerk!).

Being nosey also means learning how to make candles just because you want to know or researching family history for the same reason.

It does not give you permission to be rude. Don't insert yourself into conversations where you aren't welcome with the excuse that you're feeding your creativity.

Sure, be nosey, but be discreet and courteous too.

Jen Nipps

NOTES

Pay the rent.

Sometimes creativity seems to be more of a luxury than a necessary way of life. It's true that if you have money problems or any other significant source of stress, you're much less likely to feel or do anything creative.

It is important that you pay the bills and take care of your finances so you can afford to indulge in your creative pursuits.

Don't ignore the possibility of using your creativity to help pay the rent. This is particularly true if you sew and can take in mending or commissions. There are many other pursuits that lend themselves to freelancing and accepting commissions as well.

Anything you can do to help pay the rent will indirectly benefit your creativity.

Jen Nipps

When you have to work, make it fun.

Confucius said, "Choose a job you love, and you will never have to work a day in your life."

There have been several variations on this quote said by different people. It bears repetition and paraphrasing because it's true. No matter what kind of job you have, there are opportunities, no matter how small, to inject a little fun into it.

For example, I do medical transcription. I have for 12 years. To my way of thinking, there is no way to make that job fun.

Oh, but there is!

Within the medical problems I hear about, I could find things to inflict on my characters in my novels and short stories. And I have. I gave one character seizures after a head injury where he was hit on the back of his head with the butt of an axe. (He was wearing a primitive helmet, so it wasn't as bad as it otherwise could have been.)

Even if it's thinking outside of the box and brainstorming or cluster-mapping the solution to a problem, you can make it fun and bring a little creativity into it.

Read magazines.

It's true that magazines talk about things that are already trending, already on the cutting edge. It doesn't matter. You still need to know what is going on, what is out there. By reading magazines, you can get a good idea about that.

Keep in mind, though, that magazines are generally three months ahead of where we are now. It is to your advantage to pay attention. It's possible that an article, a quiz, or a picture can trigger something in you to create something new or improve on something discussed in the magazine.

Maybe next time it could be your idea that we see in your favorite periodical.

Watch TV.

This sounds counterintuitive to encouraging creativity. It operates under the same idea as reading magazines, though.

You see what is trending, what other people are doing, and what you might be able to duplicate or improve on. The main difference? Where magazines are a few months old, TV is immediate. Take advantage of it.

This even gives you an excuse to watch those cheesy infomercials that you secretly like to watch but don't want to get caught.

Listen to music.

They say music soothes the savage beast, but no one ever said the savage beast is you.

I'm not implying that there is anything savage or beastly about any of us. If you think about it, though, there are times when we tend to get caught up in the busy-ness of everyday life. Music can help us slow down, give us time to think, and let us catch our breath.

In those times, we allow ourselves to daydream, to generate ideas. To be creative.

For this to work in that way for me, the music generally has to be slower, quieter, and often without lyrics. It doesn't have to be classical music, but that is definitely conducive to what I'm talking about here. Even jazz can be beneficial. (I have to admit, though, if the music is too slow and/or quiet, it has been known to put me to sleep rather than allowing for creative thoughts to rise to the surface.)

Jen Nipps

Sunset Tree

Turn the radio off.

Ah. Silence.

As much as music can be a good thing, sometimes you need silence in order to hear yourself think.

We surround ourselves with noise, whether it's actual noise from external sources like traffic, people talking, kids playing, or the radio or TV on in the background or whether it's electronic noise from computers, smart phones, or eBook readers. Sometimes we just need to turn it all off, including the radio.

From time to time, we need more than just the few minutes of silence we give ourselves by turning off the radio, TV, and smart phone. Sometimes we need a whole block of silence, perhaps in the morning, where we can work without interruption.

It is in these times that I am the most surprised by how much work I am able to get done. Without intrusion from other outside sources, save for my computer or whatever I am working on, my mind is free from extra clutter. An odd sort of synergy seems to happen, letting more work, more creating, more thinking get done that what would ordinarily be possible.

Sometimes multitasking is detrimental to what we are doing and silence could be the way to go.

Let there be a few minutes of silence.

Take pictures.

This is different from taking pictures of your progress that we talked about earlier in this book.

For this one, I would encourage you to get a camera and take pictures. A camera on your phone will work in a pinch, but it's better if you have an actual camera.

Taking pictures forces us to pay attention to what we're looking at. It makes us look at things in a different way. Sometimes the frame (of the camera lens) around the thing we're photographing makes us look at a creative issue in a different way.

It is by looking at things differently that we create new ways of thinking, thus opening ourselves up to increased creativity whether in our jobs or in our lives. Or both.

Find a mentor.

A mentor is not an official teacher. Rather, they are someone who shows you the ropes and who, in some cases, you emulate. They may or may not know they are your mentor.

What do you look for in a mentor?

- Someone who knows what they are doing.
- Someone who has had success in the field you are wanting to be in.
- Someone who is willing to answer your questions and/or point you in the right direction.
- Someone who is not afraid to tell you to try it on your own.

It seems obvious to say "Someone who knows what they are doing." Trust me. It's not as obvious as it seems. There are some people who honestly luck into their success. As a result, they reap the benefits but don't know how to go about the proper process that ensures continued success.

Be careful of people who want to charge you for their mentoring. I'm not saying to never pay, but be smart and be aware. Some people are, unfortunately, out to benefit themselves at any cost to others.

Don't be one of those others.

Read books in your area of interest.

This is tricky. Just because you read books about gardening and you're a gardener doesn't automatically mean you'll be a better one. You have to read the right books for you.

If you're starting out, yes, read the beginner's guides. If, on the other hand, you've been gardening a few years, you might want to donate the beginner's books to a friend who's just getting started and move on to some more advanced books for yourself.

That doesn't mean you absolutely *can't* keep any of the beginner's books. Be selective in what you keep, though. And be choosy in what you continue to read.

Read books outside of your area of interest.

Let's face it: Reading in general makes you more of a well-rounded person with benefits in all areas of your life. Books about photography, past presidents, cooking, and more broaden your horizons and has the potential to open your mind to new ideas.

New ideas? Where do those come from?

Creativity!

Keep reading.

NOTES

Go to a museum.

Museums are treasure troves for creativity.

It doesn't matter whether it is an art museum, a natural science museum, or a war museum, among many others. What matters is how you approach it.

If you adopt an attitude of "just another boring museum," you miss the point.

Museums celebrate accomplishments in art, science, technology, and more! Don't go in thinking that you will be bored by the art or by the "nerdy science stuff." Go in wondering what you will find that will inspire you.

Ask yourself a few questions:

- o What is the point of this exhibit?
- o Did it meet its point or not?
- o What could be done differently for it to achieve its purpose more effectively?

Don't be afraid to take notes. Let it simmer in your subconscious before you consider the trip a failure or a waste of time.

Go to the library.

If museums are treasure troves of creativity, libraries are its archives.

Browsing for your favorite subject might show you what is missing in its coverage. Take note of it. That might be a need you can fill through your own writing, art, photography, or music.

For the books that *are* available, check some out. Is the coverage in the book adequate? There might be a niche in the subject matter in a book itself that is outdated or simply not there.

Once again, take notes. Let it provide more fuel for the slow burn of your creativity.

Go to a nightclub.

Chances are, if you regularly go to nightclubs, this might not work for you. It won't be a new environment.

Now, with that said, yes, go to a nightclub. I know you'll be going to have fun, to party, but pay attention, too. What kind of music is playing? What are some of the more outrageous outfits?

More importantly, how can you use this to feed your creativity?

Noticing some of the following will help.
Clothes
Colors
Music tempo
Music volume

Challenge yourself to use something from this in your current (or next) project.

Read the newspaper.

Let me guess. You're thinking "boring" or "snooze-fest."

You might be right. On the other hand, you might not be. If you just look at the main section with its dry news and crime reports, it can be rather boring. What about the Lifestyles section? Sports? Those areas of the paper are usually more engaging, even entertaining.

In order for your creativity to be relevant to your community, town, or state, you need to know what's going on. You need to be able to have a way to put your finger on the pulse of what's trending, what's popular. No, this doesn't mean that you chase trends. It does mean you know which end is up and why you are doing what you do.

Even if your paper is a weekly, it's important to know what's going on, so read it.

Exercise your body.

If you were to look at me, you would laugh that I would have the audacity to suggest you exercise. Obviously, you don't have to. It's a tip, not a law. Not only that, it really can help you develop your creative muscle, so to speak.

How?

Let me use myself as an example. If I have access to a relatively flat surface (not the rutted country road I currently live on), I like to go for walks. Since I am primarily a writer, I tend to have conversations with my characters or with the subject at hand, if it's a nonfiction piece. Otherwise, I notice how nature combines colors in unexpected ways. It isn't unheard of for me to take these color combinations back to my crochet or knitting.

And this is all because I appeared to be exercising.

Bottles on Display

Gain a different perspective.

When is the last time you stood on your head?

For many of us, that isn't physically possible. So what's the next best thing to help you get a different perspective on a situation or subject matter?

Get your camera and go outside. (In this case, the camera on your mobile phone will do fine. These pictures are for your eyes only.)

Take a picture of a tree just straight-on. There's nothing unusual about that. Now, go right up to the tree and stand by the trunk. Take a picture looking *up* into the branches, a close-up of the bark, down through some branches, or even down the tree to the grass and roots.

How has your perspective changed?

Do the same thing with several other things. Once, I took pictures of a fire hydrant. The first one looked down on it from a distance. Another looked at it from a bird's-eye view, straight overhead. The next one was what I called a dog's-eye view. I got on my knees to get that shot and it was definitely a different perspective.

After a few minutes of getting a different perspective through pictures, you can take that process back to your current project and figure out a new perspective that might enhance what you currently have going.

Learn a new skill.

When we learn something, we are changing the pathways in our brain. When we change the way we think in this way, we open ourselves up to more creativity.

It doesn't matter *what* we are learning, just that we *are* learning. I have described myself on more than one occasion as an eternal student. Anyone who practices any kind of creative act should be. A favorite quote of mine is one I made up:

Live and learn or get brain rot.

It's not a pretty picture. What I mean by "brain rot" can best be described as having made a decision that you no longer need to learn. By not learning anything new, you risk losing some of your mental capacity, some of your brain power.

Some of your creativity.

Don't do that. Make a point to continue learning and adding to your skillset.

Rules are necessary so you know when you are breaking them and why.

Everything has rules. Some show us the way as we are learning something new. When we know what we are doing, sometimes they get in the way. When this happens, you can break the rules in order to grow.

Knowing the rules first is important. Otherwise, you're doing the equivalent of throwing spaghetti at the wall and seeing what sticks. That makes it difficult to repeat what you've done in order to build on it and increase your skillset.

Bending, breaking, or reshaping the rules of your preferred creative outlet let you expand your creativity and build on what you, and perhaps what others, have done before. Call it experimenting, if you prefer. Regardless, it can be quite fun.

What rules have you broken recently? None? Maybe it's time to change that.

Observe.

There is a lot we can learn from the world around us that can influence our creativity. Too often, we hurry through life without paying attention to the things we see every day. We see them, we know they're there, but we don't truly *see* them.

Slow down and really see what is around you.

Nature has some surprising color combinations and shapes without interference from man. Sometimes people even learn from that and bring it into their living spaces and work environments. And we as people ourselves can do some surprising things.

If we take a minute to truly look at, to observe, what is around us and take it in, we can let it influence our creativity and surprise ourselves with what develops.

Trust yourself.

"I can't do that because I'm not good enough."

"You're so much more creative than I am."

"I could never be a writer/artist/musician/dancer."

"I'm not a very good cook."

All of these comments, and more, have been said to me on more than one occasion. It all boils down, to use a cooking metaphor, to a bunch of baloney.

It is because they don't trust themselves. They don't trust their own creativity.

We've talked before about giving yourself permission to be creative. That's only part of it. You also have to trust yourself. I'll be honest. It isn't easy. You have to believe other people above your inner critic who is screaming that you're not any good or that you're not creative or that you can't cook....

You get the idea.

There's a small voice under the loud critic that says things like "I am good," "I am creative," and "I can cook/draw/paint/dance/play music/sing." You have to learn to listen to that inner voice of confidence, look for it behind your inner critic. Feed it by believing it and believing what good things other people have to say about your work.

Then you will begin to trust yourself.

Deal with stress before it deals with you.

A common source of creative blocks is directly related to stress. I've been there.

You have to come up with a way of dealing with stress before it deals with you. Don't let it build up to the point that you can't do anything creative. There are several ways to do this.

- o Exercise.
- o Get enough sleep.
- o Do something small related to your creativity every day.
- o Meditate.

You might find one of these ways of dealing with stress works for you. Maybe none of them will. In that case, you need to find what does work for you and stay with it. Your creativity will thank you.

NOTES

Ride a bike.

I remember the feeling of riding a bike. For me, with my eyesight, it was kind of scary, but I loved the feeling of wind in my hair. I would watch out for the potholes in the roads around our neighborhood by the way the shadows were in them. One October, after time change, I wasn't used to the shadows yet. I hit a particularly big pothole, wrecked, and cracked my elbow. When my mom found out how I saw the potholes, she made me sell my bike.

Even the idea of riding a bike is enough to generate memories and feed our creativity. Imagine what it would do if you were to actually ride one!

What is it like to you? How do you feel? Is it a heady rush or is it a scary, slow ride while you watch the pebble-flecked blacktop glide under your front wheel while you watch for potholes that like to hide from you?

Whatever it is, use the feelings, the memories, it brings to you.

Ideas are everywhere.

There are two schools of thought at play here. One says that we have to work for our ideas and they are ours alone. Another says that ideas are everywhere, available to everyone and it is what we do with them that makes them unique.

Guess which one I agree with?

If you said the second one, you're right. The first one, to my way of thinking, implies that only certain people are creative and they are the ones who can come up with the ideas. The second one suggests that everyone is creative and ideas are readily available for all of us.

Now, that is not to say that sometimes it *feels* like we are working hard to come up with our ideas. How something feels and the truth of it are not always the same. That is what allows for differing schools of thought and theories on the same subject.

Don't limit yourself by thinking ideas are only for the select few unless you believe that you are one of them.

Everyone is creative, but not everyone knows how to tap into it.

This is the key and it bears repeating.

Everyone is creative. Some of us don't know how to access our creativity. That's why some tools, like a writing practice (as mentioned before), can be beneficial to us. The act of writing, of making lists, of saying "I wish...," help you tap into your creativity whether you realize it at the time or not.

In the introduction to my book, *Devoted to Creating: Igniting the Creative Spark in Everyone*, I say I firmly believe everyone is creative. Some people don't know how to tap into it. Some people don't realize the things they do, the things they *enjoy* doing, are creative.

What do I think is creative? Writing, drawing, painting, singing, dancing, cooking, gardening, teaching, babysitting, crocheting, knitting, beading, making jewelry, anything related to arts and crafts, building things.

Creativity doesn't discriminate for age, gender, income, or form. Neither should we.

Don't let anyone tell you that you can't.

We tell ourselves negative things often enough. Don't let someone else tell you that you can't do something. I've done that.

I let someone tell me that I would never be any kind of artist. I believed it. I believed it not only for drawing and painting but for *any* kind of art. I internalized that statement and believed it for about 25 years.

It took someone telling me that I was an artist with my beadwork and my crochet to begin to believe I was an artist.

And you are too.

It doesn't matter what your medium is. If you are creating, you are an artist. Do you think a master chef is any less an artist than a master artist in acrylics? Each is an artist in their own way. The chef's medium just happens to be food and serving dishes rather than brushes, paint, and canvas.

Just as you wouldn't tell someone else they couldn't do something, don't let someone else tell you that either.

If someone does tell you that you can't, prove them wrong.

Nobody knows what you can or cannot do other than you. Because of that, no one knows if you can do any particular artistic or creative project other than you until you try it.

On a related note, trying something one time is not a good indicator of if you can do it or not. What would it have been like if Picasso stopped after his first try at painting? Or Da Vinci? The Wright brothers?

There are many advancements in art, architecture, science, medicine, and more because those people didn't let someone else tell them they couldn't do it.

It said that Thomas Edison "failed" 1,000 times before he succeeded in inventing the light bulb. It's also said that he disagreed and said the process had that many steps.

No one is perfect on the first try. No one can say "you can't" after one try. Don't let them do it.

Up the Tree

Conclusion

I'm sure you've guessed by now that there are a lot more creativity tips that I haven't included here. There are several reasons for that. One of them is that since you now know what kinds of things to do, what kinds of questions to ask yourself, you don't need me to ask them for you.

However, if you find that you want more creativity coaching than what is available in this book, I am available for coaching sessions starting at $40 an hour. You can e-mail me at jen@jen-nipps.com for more information about that. Just include "Creativity Coaching" in the subject line.

Also feel free to like the Creative Tips Facebook page. www.facebook.com/creativitytips. Join the discussion there, ask questions, and share your own tips.

About the Author

Jen Nipps writes from her home in Oklahoma. She is an award-winning poet and author. She has a wide variety of interests that influence her writing. She gives presentations on various topics related to writing, creativity, social media, and blogging. She is working toward being a certified creativity coach and offers creativity consulting/coaching services.

Other Books by Jen Nipps

Get "Twitter"pated: A Writer's Handbook to Twitter
Published by CreateSpace/JEN Enterprises

Windsong & Other Poems
Published by CreateSpace/JEN Enterprises

Devoted to Creating: Igniting the Creative Spark in Everyone
Published by Devoted Books
Navajo Rose

(written as Kat O'Reilly)
Published by CreateSpace/GenXt Books

Connect with Jen Online

Website	http://www.jen-nipps.com
Blog	http://blog.jen-nipps.com
Facebook	http://www.facebook.com/byjennipps
Twitter	http://www.twitter.com/jennipps

Jen Nipps

Jen Nipps